R62397

PC-2976
£19.99

Bus Stop

D1610400

WITHDRAWN FROM STOCK

This was the first Bus Stop shop on London's Kensington Church Street. It had been an old-fashioned grocer's called Cullum's, with Victorian mahogany wall fittings. These were left in place to give the store a colourful atmosphere. Bus Stop lettering was based on that of the old signage.

Bus Stop

*and the influence of the 70s
on fashion today*

A SCRAPBOOK

Lee Bender

A & C BLACK • LONDON

746.
92092
BEN

All drawings and Bus Stop clothes by Lee Bender

Text written by Lee Bender and Graham Cadwallader

I dedicate this book to Cecil, with love – Lee

My special thanks to Graham Cadwallader for suggesting that I write and illustrate this book about Bus Stop, and for his very generous help with the writing of the text. I thank him, also, for photographs of all the accessories.

Thanks, too, to Mary Boyle who was my assistant in the early years of Bus Stop and who reminded me of incidents in the workplace that I had forgotten; and to Jean Macleod for jogging my memory about past fun times at Bus Stop.

Thanks to Mark Eastment of the Victoria & Albert Museum for seeing the potential in my material, for all his assistance and encouragement, and for introducing me to Linda Lambert of A & C Black; thanks to Linda for accepting my proposal and also to Anne Watts for her work as editor.

Thanks to Georgina Linhart, for helping me to publicise the book.

And I must here acknowledge the supply of photographs by the following photographers and newspapers/ magazines:

Brian Aris: p. 16 Joan Collins | David Bailey: p. 44 pink satin frill top | Shirley Beljon: p. 15 Lee and team | Mike Berkofsky: p. 93 striped blouse | John Bishop: p. 73 tartan check jacket and black shorts | *Brides* (*Vogue*): p. 138 Bus Stop bride *c*1974 | *Daily Record*: p. 59 white satin shorts and elasticised bandeau; shorts, shirt and coolie hat | Robert Freeson (courtesy of Freeson Mason Gallery): p. 35 Verushka (2 pictures) | *Grattan* catalogue: p. 21 long tunic sweaters; p. 22 plaid coat and jumpsuit; p. 25 sweater, gloves and scarf; p. 39 black jumpsuit; p. 40 two-piece and jumpsuit in velvet; p. 51 Fair Isle sweater; p. 63 jumpsuit on 1976 catalogue; p. 77 crepe top and skirt with frill; p. 79 floral two-piece and silky duo; p. 81 white print jersey dress; p. 98 striped and checked suits; p. 103 beaver fake-fur jacket; pp 112-13 khaki culotte dress/jumpsuit; p. 129 two dresses, of jersey and velvet; p. 130 jersey print dress/white wool jacket; p. 131 check wool four-piece; p. 134 70s' tea dress | © Sian Irvine: p. 26 black strawberry sweater | © Saul Leiter (courtesy Howard Greenberg Gallery NYC): p. 73 long yellow tartan skirt; p. 75 three-piece trouser suit | *Newcastle Evening Chronicle*: p. 80 two girls in tea dresses, 1975 | Helmut Newton (courtesy of Helmut Newton Foundation): cover picture and p. 47 red satin shorts and blouson | Harri Peccinotti: p. 23 knit playsuit; biker sweater; p. 30 jersey jacket; p. 32 striped jersey tops; p. 33 two jersey outfits | Christa Peters, who took many photos for Bus Stop: p. 37 lurex zipper jacket; p. 38 lurex dress; one-shoulder dress with white jacquard; p. 39 pink and black stripe dress *à la Marilyn Monroe*; p. 40 circular skirt and lurex sweater; p. 41 black ciré dress; p. 46 khaki satin jodhpurs and jacket; p. 48 white satin playsuits; p. 60 lurex bikinis; p. 65 cheesecloth jumpsuit; p. 94 zigzag knit coat; zigzag sweater; p. 95 bouclé striped sweater; p. 140 70s' one-shoulder lurex sweater | POSH Vintage, USA: p. 141 Bus Stop designs on website | *The Sunday Times* magazine: p. 46 clown in striped satin dungarees; p. 47 clown in baggy satin trousers with satin printed top; p. 55 Barbara Bach in Viva Maria outfit; p. 57 Barbara Bach in top and shorts | Homer Sykes: back cover photo of author | *Vogue*: p. 104 fake lambskin coat

Photographs have been collected over the years – the source of some of them is unknown.

First published 2010
A & C Black Publishers Limited
36 Soho Square
London W1D 3QY

ISBN 978 14081 1142 0

Copyright © 2010 Lee Bender

Lee Bender has asserted her rights under the Copyright, Design and Patents Act, 1988, to be identified as the author of this work.

A CIP catalogue record for this book is available from the British Library.

All rights reserved. No part of this publication may be reproduced in any form or by any means – graphic, electronic or mechanical, including photocopying, recording, taping or information storage and retrieval systems – without the prior permission in writing of the publishers.

Typeset in 11 on 14pt Myriad Light
Book design by Susan McIntyre
Cover design by James Watson

Printed and bound by Star Standard, Singapore

A & C Black uses paper produced with elemental chlorine-free pulp, harvested from managed sustainable sources.

Contents

"Society style in scintillating satin creations"

"Demure new dresses for Duchesses and debutantes"

STAND OUT AT ASCOT AND HENLEY

HIGHLIGHTS OF THE SUMMER FROM THE HAUTE COUTURE HOUSE OF HARTNELL

Life before Bus Stop. Headlines from contemporary fashion magazines.

Chapter One

Before Bus Stop

England was, for the 50s and 60s and many years before, in a drab era of clothing choices for the majority of girls and women. Fashions for individuals were rare.

The Paris twice-yearly collections catered for the lucky few who could afford the steep prices. Only at the upper end of the social spectrum, in the world of *haute couture*, was there much attention paid to style. Ready-to-wear clothes were generally a poor woman's version of those worn by the wealthy. Copies of designer originals were produced for the following season by an assortment of manufacturers in commercial imitation.

It must also be said that it became an era of 'copycat fashion'. When a new fashion came in, women rushed out to buy it and weren't concerned that they all looked the same as each other. In fact, what was important was that they all had to have it.

Mix-and-match co-ordinated clothes were unheard of – customers had to find different shops for skirts, dresses, coats, knitwear, jackets and accessories.

There were really only two 'looks' – dressed up and dressed down. This made choosing wardrobes very simple. No mixing up of looks, so unlike today's cutting-edge scene.

This was an England where 'fashion' essentially meant exclusiveness, elegance and the monied classes: costly, tailor-made chic from such designers as Dior, Balenciaga, Laroche, Givenchy, Balmain, Hardy Amies and Norman Hartnell. Clothes were designed to be worn at Ascot, Wimbledon, Henley and at coming-out balls for well-heeled debutantes.

Little couture establishments and made-to-measure private dressmakers were on call. There were a few large-scale manufacturers such as Marks & Spencers, but these suppliers had to design and manufacture their merchandise in mass production. There was no room for the short and ever-changing fashion deadlines later to be met by the newly emerging wave of 'youth' boutiques.

What about the new crowds of young, exuberant and daredevil girls from more ordinary backgrounds? They were longing to express their own individuality in their own fashion statements: they wanted cheap, cheerful and stylish clothes, which they could easily change according to the mood of the moment and the season of the year – and throw away. Nobody could supply such outfits and top-to-toe co-ordinates, they simply didn't exist!

Bus Stop's whole *raison d'être* was to bypass such upper-crust styles as those shown and spearhead a new dimension in the lives of perhaps less privileged girls. Designer styling at prices everyone could manage, and a pretty trendy Bus Stop label in the lining as well!

Bus Stop helped to pioneer what was then seen as revolution, although nowadays evolution would seem to be a more accurate description. Bus Stop provided a world of all-together glamour, craziness and party party party euphoria, a world where it didn't matter how expensive or inexpensive your clothes were. What mattered was how well Bus Stop provided you with clothes that made you feel just as you wanted to look and be like.

Producing this whole new change in dressing lifestyle was what Bus Stop was all about. Letting the Bus Stop girls of the 70s in on the weird and wonderful world of the new landmarks of fashion was a serious departure from the sophisticated, aristocratic mindset of earlier decades and generations.

"Designer styling at easy-to-afford prices!"

This was Bus Stop's fundamental 'mission statement', and this is what turned Bus Stop into so revolutionary/evolutionary a presence in London, all over the UK and in countries throughout the world.

The whole purpose of Bus Stop was to pioneer a revolution in the lives of the average girl. The intention was to produce designer styling at affordable prices for everyone.

A little 50s' nostalgia

And think of the stars of that time: Elizabeth Taylor, Rita Hayworth, Audrey Hepburn and Grace Kelly!

Trapeze line dress, 1958

Circular skirts

Court shoes all the rage

Cigarette holder

50s' tunic and skirt – all dressed up for Henley Regatta, tennis at Wimbledon and cocktails at the Ritz

Stately home

Chanel in the 50s

One of the greatest designers of the twentieth century, long before Bus Stop, and a huge influence, was Gabrielle Chanel. In the 20s, she invented the flat-chested, boyish *garçonne* look. Later came superbly simple navy-and-white jersey cardigan suits, made with handsome linings and pockets to hold cigarettes and keys. Skirts had pleats, suits were in muted colours and of studied simplicity. Slingback shoes had pointed black toes. Heavy gold chains and glass bead necklaces were all part of the *gamine* signature look. The quilted Chanel bag with chain handles is, of course, still with us today.

Chanel suit

Beaded cardigan

In those days, couture and couturiers were the reserve of the upper crust – living in Mayfair and Belgravia, and enjoying large and opulent partying weekends in country houses. Double-barrelled names headed this élite, the ladies with impeccable sartorial taste.

Tiaras

A commonplace piece of aristocratic headgear during the period – usually worn without too many tantrums!

Gowns with long floor-sweeping trains

Many of the social functions of that era featured positively in Hollywood production numbers, with processions and with attendants deployed to carry the trains of such resplendent gowns. Actually, did Cannes 2009 look so much different?

Chapter Two

The birth of Bus Stop

Fashion is a field of incessant experimentation and unending change. Everything is transient, and it's a matter of opinion whether you are 'in' or 'out', 'yes' or 'yesterday'.

When the 60s drew to a close and the early 70s dawned, the age of promiscuity and newly found freedom for the young came bursting on the scene.

The times had already started to change. In science. In music. Rock music performances were no longer confined to youth clubs but staged on a massive open-air scale in ginormous new outdoor and indoor concert venues.

Bus Stop had the opportunity to promote new daring styles and colours, not only in clothing but also in accessories. Mix-and-match and co-ordinating looks could all be bought by the shoppers for the wholesale prices that Bus Stop managed to charge because the products were made by Bus Stop in their own factories, with no middlemen. What fun was to be had! A few pounds would buy you a bagful of clothing to be worn for a week or two. And you could then come back and buy another bagful two weeks later for very little money. What a shame those times and prices are not around now!

What a landmark of a year 1969 turned out to be – the last year, of course, of the so-called Swinging Sixties. Buzz Aldrin and the American NASA team walked on the moon and sent photos back to Mission Control on earth. Hippies in flower power costume made their first appearance all over the world, in keeping with the Scott McKenzie anthem, 'If you're going to San Francisco'. Jimi Hendrix played guitar and sang 'Purple Haze' with unrivalled dexterity, and Frank Zappa and the Mothers of Invention were at the height of their popularity and power. The Beatles were recording 'Come together' and George Harrison's 'Something in the way she moves'. Joan Baez, Janis Joplin and Bob Dylan were in full voice and force.

There were crowds of thousands at the rock festivals of Woodstock and Glastonbury. The Rolling Stones held an eventful gig in Altamont, California, with Hell's Angels doubling as their bodyguards. Dennis Hopper's counter-culture biker movie *Easy Rider*, with Jack Nicholson and Peter Fonda, was a massive hit at the box office, and Dustin Hoffman and Jon Voight starred in the influential *Midnight Cowboy*. The whole world was in a state of upheaval and Bus Stop had every intention of adding yet more creativity to the cultural maelstrom.

How Bus Stop started: a fashion designer's notes, sketches and photos

When Bus Stop set up shop in Kensington Church Street in 1969, fashion fans were in a quandary. At that time, fashion companies and designers specialised in making skirts, or knitwear, or suits, or coats, or dresses. Co-ordinates had never been envisaged before 1969. Nor were the public used to buying matching clothes all under one roof. So the design of everything to mix and match was an overriding ambition, with a store able to display and sell co-ordinates together on the same premises. And that's exactly what happened.

Lee and son

Flagship store, Kensington

Bus Stop tops, jackets, coats, sweaters, the whole lot: they were manufactured in Bus Stop factories as matching ensembles, with trousers, skirts and dresses, even accessories, all to be combined or worn separately.

Bus Stop began with some way-out new ready-to-wear outfits – with special attention given to sexy, never-ending party clothes with a difference, that could be paraded anytime during the day and evening. An unheard-of experiment in 1969 – and what a dream!

Opening day

I rushed in with the Hoover first thing in the morning, only to find a massive queue of the kind later to be associated with Bus Stop stores all over Britain. Of course, we hadn't made enough stock. Once the crowd had managed to get in, we were cleared out within a few hours. We had to do some rethinking so that we could refill the rails quickly and efficiently. What a task, and what a rush. But we did it, and all the factories were working day and night for several months until we caught up with demand.

Over the next ten years, Bus Stop became a legend.

How I worked

I worked differently from most designers. At the start of each season it was time to sit down and work out the colours and shapes, *before* visiting the fabric exhibitions. This was because it cut down the hours spent looking at endless fabrics in the huge display halls. After a few hours of walking and looking at fabrics, I tire and can no longer concentrate on the job in hand. So I adopted the idea of working out my colours and designs beforehand. Then I sampled only fabrics which fitted my pre-conceived plans. No more exhaustion and confusion!

I am always surprised when designers tell me that they need to visit the fabric exhibitions for ideas before making their plans. In Paris and in Germany, where the exhibitions are huge, there are umpteen halls to visit. This can drag on for days and, after a morning's viewing, one has just about switched off.

To get design ideas, you have to be in 'design mode' in your head. With the sample room waiting for your sketches, when your back is against the wall, when you're running out of time … that's when the best work is produced.

I might, for instance, be driving behind a lorry painted in unusual colours. Suddenly the colours looked *new* to me. This could set me off on a whole new way of thinking, and bring amazing new fabric and colour combination results. I might also scour the antique markets in London and Paris for tops and dresses of the 30s and 40s, in order to have attractive prints made from them. Then I could give them to a fabric printer to adapt and print onto crepe de chine and soft fluid fabrics, in my new season's colours. The fabrics were ideal for the glam and dressy party looks that Bus Stop was renowned for creating.

Wrap print top and wrap satin skirt

There were 8–10 of us working in the sample room:

- Sample Room Manager
- 2–3 Pattern Cutters
- 4–5 Samples Machinists
- 1 Sample Cutter (to cut out the garments)
- and me, overseeing it all

When the samples were costed, finished and ready to be seen, we would hold a design meeting with the production manager and assistants. We would decide, first of all, if we wanted to show them as part of a collection. If so, we would decide on the printing, fabrics and timing.

We would then order fabrics and have first samples made by our factories. The process of making up the garments would begin. We would make a small amount of stock first, ascertain how it sold and repeat quickly the best styles and colours. Cloth left over would be cut into another winning style.

The Bus Stop team in the studio above the Kensington Church Street store. All wearing Bus Stop clothes.
From left to right: Belinda, manageress; me; Alli, assistant manageress; Carol, buying assistant

Meanwhile I would show the collection in the studio to the newspapers and magazines. After the new collections arrived in the shops, customers came rushing in, all fighting for the new stock.

We were inundated by all kinds of well-known people, the celebrities of the time, who came to buy designer looks at what were incredibly cheap prices. Bus Stop clothes came straight out of factory – into shop!

Ready-to-wear designers had never received any of the stardom of today's designers – but from now on we had an unparalleled opportunity to shake the fashion kaleidoscope.

Famous customers included:

Brigitte Bardot, Vanessa Redgrave, Charlotte Rampling, Lauren Bacall, Patti Boyd, Nina Simone, Marianne Faithfull, Angela Bowie, Joanna Lumley, Joan Collins, Jilly Cooper and, indeed, a whole roll-call of the characters who made up the decade of the 70s. In fact, all the customers visiting London would at once make a beeline for Bus Stop, as we were continually changing our stock.

Joan Collins – one of Bus Stop's most enthusiastic customers

Daughter of a London theatrical booking agent, she made her stage debut in *The Doll's House* at the age of nine. She went on to theatre, film and tv stardom, most famously in *Dynasty*, winning a Golden Globe along the way.

'Lee Bender has always been a favourite designer of mine,' she said in the 70s.

'She designs clothes for ladies with boobs and bums.'

'Her Bus Stop stores are filled with individual high-fashion looks, but sell at a fraction of the price you find in other top shops.'

Joan Collins wearing yellow jumpsuit in the Daily Star

SUPERBITCH, SUPERGLOSS

Nobody gets the better of sexy Joan Collins

SHE'S slick. She's stylish. She's a superbitch.
Nobody gets the better of Joan Collins.
If she can't bully you, she'll seduce you with her charm.
Even Father Time has surrendered.
Those glossy good looks that turned men weak at the knees in the 'fifties are still with her.
As the song says it's the way she walks, it's the way she talks. And that means one thing . . . SEX APPEAL.
When it comes to clothes, there isn't a thing that this luscious lady doesn't know. From buying blazers in Paris to sliding into her 16-year-old daughter's jeans.
"Being a Gemini, darling.

I wear clothes according to how I feel when I wake up in the morning," she says.
"Lee Bender has always been a favourite designer of mine. She designs clothes for ladies with boobs and bums.
"Her stores, Bus Stop, are filled with individual high fashion looks but sell at a fraction of the price you find in other top shops.

Sported

"I'm really into the 50s at the moment, darling." As she spoke, she slipped into a waist-clinching belt that probably hasn't moved a notch since she sported that particular look first time round!
Joan Collins's film, The Bitch, is due for its London premiere on May 19.
If the film is anything like the real Joan Collins, it's bound to be an outrageous success.

Fashion special by SANDY WILLIAMS

Joan Collins wearing brown jumpsuit in the Daily Star

Bus Stop, Kensington – the shop interior

Bus Stop was known all over town for its devotion to bright red decoration. We chose the name because London buses were bright red and red was always one of my favourite colours. (In Chinese circles it means auspicious good luck.) Telephone boxes and postboxes were bright red, too, and we wanted to make sure that Bus Stop was a place you regularly stopped at – very 'swinging London'.

This convivial approach was in total contrast to the clinical, minimalist approach to shop design then prevalent all over smart shops in London. The Bus Stop shop originally accommodated a Victorian grocer. What we wanted to do was to give it the feeling of a cheery, informal, casual Victorian pub!

The picture below was the small counter at the back of the shop. As you can see we had a mish-mash of jewellery, feathers, baskets of flowers to pin on a lapel or a hat. Badges and brooches were worn on lapels several at a time. There were belts, bags, hats and scarves as well, in fact every kind of accessory we could lay our hands on.

Inside the Bus Stop, Kensington, store

Small counter at the back of the shop

Bus Stop clothes in the Kensington store

Badges of Marilyn Monroe, Campbell's tomato soup and other icons were worn on lapels several at a time.

Perfume bottle brooch

Face brooch

Assorted brooches

Adam Ant made us our jewellery, in resin. He produced all the 'pin-up' film stars, all kinds of fruit, teddy bears and plenty of other amusing designs. He was in art college at the time and this was his 'off-duty' way of making money. We kept selling out his jewellery and we kept him very busy for ages.

We were also lucky in finding someone who made little purses and bags in bright leathers and suedes, edged in natural coloured braid, which we used to order in hundreds.

It was all self-service at Bus Stop. No more girls to hound and pester you. Just fifteen to twenty girls per shop, to make sure you got the clothes you really wanted. We had small brass rails made to display the clothes, in keeping with the interior of the shops.

Communal changing room, too – unheard of in fashion boutiques until the early 70s. 75% of our customers were young, and didn't mind changing in a crowd of other customers. Their mums got quite used to it in time! Even famous personages were happy to try clothes on in the changing room – such was the new spirit of freedom and the stampede to buy the clothes. I remember an occasion when an Italian TV crew came to Bus Stop to film the

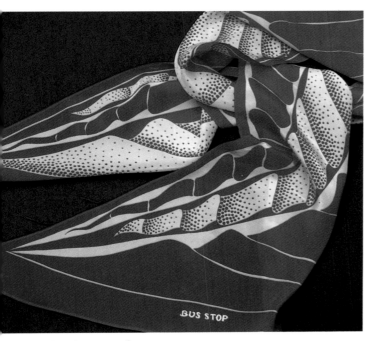

Bus Stop scarf

Me and my husband Cecil

shop. They were forbidden to go into the changing room. But who, of course, could stop them? Screams of panic at once followed. And in equal panic we somehow managed to extricate them! How difficult was that?

We were a team

The running of Bus Stop had a clear division. I did all the designing and my husband Cecil was the business brain. I and my assistant were responsible for the choice of fabrics and for the seeking of the million and one other products and accessories that we bought in or had made especially for us.

I spent a major part of the day checking new samples made from my sketches, working with the pattern cutter and the machinists, and trying on the samples.

I have a firm belief that by trying everything on myself, rather than by trying it on a gorgeous model of ideal proportions, I can *feel* if it is roomy enough under the arms. Also, I can see if it makes me feel fat or look fat. One cannot help but be amazed to notice that even stick-thin females – when trying on clothes in a shop – worry about the clothes making them look fat.

Me and the model

Teamwork in action

Once the special production patterns had been made from the first sample, they were handed to the production manager together with a workroom sample and a graded set of patterns. Then they were sent to the factories to be cut out and sewn, and a counter sample was made.

We had a few small favourite makers-up, who used to make pretty lingerie, bikinis, wallets, little bags and purses. All very young and girlie and just for us. They would bring us samples, and we would give them small orders. We then had something exclusive that no other shop had.

We would also deal with large manufacturers, from whom we would buy accessories such as hats, berets, belts, bags, jewellery, shoes, fruit and flowers that could be pinned on. We also ordered special tights and stockings in our own colours, to match the clothes. We bought anything that attracted us that we could sell and displayed the smaller things on a long counter in the shop

I loved to spend Saturday afternoons in the Kensington shop, serving behind the counter. It was fascinating to watch the hordes of customers coming in, seeing what they wore and often recognising a famous person. We didn't bother anybody. People could just pick up what they liked and team outfits together themselves, without any interference. We would offer help only when they wanted it. I noticed we even had a lot of pre-teens coming in with their mums and, curiously, both generations found plenty of clothes they wanted. I remember serving Lauren Bacall myself. She must have liked the clothes, because she went out with six large red Bus Stop bags.

Production work in action

The essential procedure was always the same. We would arrive at our factories with the workroom samples and lengths of fabric for copies to be made. Sometimes the results weren't quite 100% satisfactory and we would have to go back to the factory and work with the staff there until perfection was achieved.

I very much enjoyed visits to Milan and Florence. We worked there with two factories that made knitwear and T-shirts. They would provide us with jersey knit fabric and bits of ribbing, and we would make up a rough sweater in our sample room to see how the style would look. We then gave the sample to the factory to be made up into a further sample.

My husband Cecil dealt with production, the finding of shop locations and the looking-after of the endless day-to-day routine problems of running a countrywide business. Fabric had to be ordered, factories had to be monitored, and staff had to be dealt with not only in head office but in all the shops.

Because Bus Stop was such a sure-fire success in London from the start, Cecil and I were most interested in seeing if the boutique would do equally well in other cities in Britain.

We soon opened one of our most successful stores in Glasgow, quickly followed by that in Edinburgh. In the end we were to have twelve shops in the UK, various shops-within- stores in the USA and Canada, Hong Kong and Japan, and also various other wholesale customers from abroad. Life was certainly busy for Cecil.

Chapter Three

Bus Stop and bright colours

t was also a time of experimentation with colour and fabrics.

As 'good taste' – as we knew it – flew out of the window, bright colours could for once be worn together for clashing effect. This gave us designers enormous opportunities to create a new kind of look, with colour, wild prints, spots and checks mixed together in a variety of different materials.

Different types of fabrics were also experimented with. I used soft crepes and satins, towelling and jerseys, designing everything possible to look semi-dressy, so that the clothes would be multi-functional and positively easy to sell.

*Long tunic
sweaters*

Plaid coat and jumpsuit

Knit playsuit

In the early 70s, Bus Stop entered into a challenging time of exploration – akin to what was going on all over the world of art, fashion and music. There was the increasing popularity of cars painted at their owner's commission – with tailor-made new pop art designs, such as the earlier masterwork that was John Lennon's Rolls Royce.

Allen Jones, the artist, was producing truly sexy, colourful and faintly risqué sculptures such as tables supported by alluring semi-naked ladies in high boots. David Hockney was painting canvases of Californian swimming pools in muted Technicolor.

Biker sweater

Bob Marley was singing colourful Jamaican reggae, such as 'No Woman No Cry'. Carlos Santana's songs – 'Black Magic Woman', 'Oye Como Va' – were full of vibrant, lyrical South American passion.

Bus Stop now began to bring out sultry and explosive designs – in satins, velvets, sequin-studded fabrics, lurex and exhibitionist patterns.

Red crochet hat and scarf

Red crochet top to match

Art deco printed blouse with floppy collar

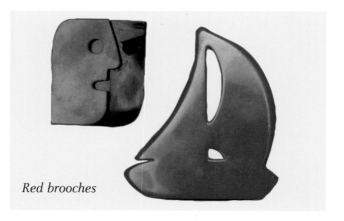

Red brooches

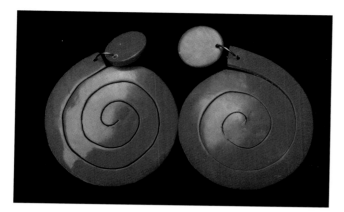

Round red earrings

Knit tank top and bolero
with lurex added

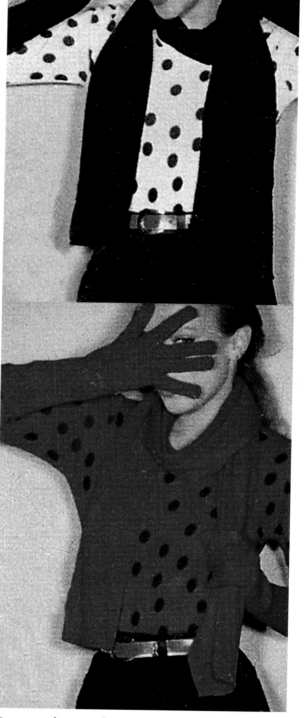

Sweater, gloves and scarf

Bus Stop black strawberry sweater

We sold large numbers of platform shoes in mixed primary colours and – a whizzbang popular number – the eye-catching Bus Stop strawberry jackets. Clothes like these reached full bloom a little later on, in the Glam Rock era, but in the early 70s they marked a real turning point after a period of much more sombre fashion.

Strawberry sweater and cherry cardigan

Silk and rayon two-piece

Strawberry jacket with satin trousers

Strawberry earrings

Matching brights

In 1971–72 colours of clothing had become brighter and more vibrant in general fashion and at Bus Stop. Shoes followed suit, in similar style and spirit. Cars were customised and decorated in all shades and patterns, and related well to the multi-coloured clothes.

Platform shoes, customised cars and T-shirts so colourful they'd become almost blinding.

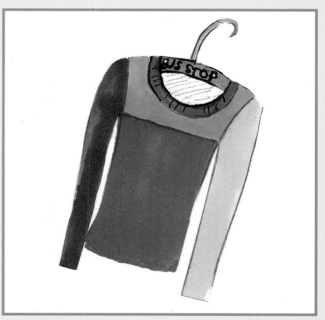

All in clashing colours worn together – 70s' brights

Brights

This multi-stripe long T-shirt and leggings had matching plain shorts and cardigan. You could wear it then and you could be wearing it now. Not so very much has changed in thirty-five years.

A customised car in similar colours

Mix-and-match jersey lines from 1972 ~ from Northern Ireland

In the early 70s we began to have jersey separates made in Northern Ireland. There was one occasion when Cecil made a working visit to a factory in Belfast. He went to see a company who made thousands of our various styles of jersey and T-shirt tops for us.

The particular factory specialised in a very fine plain and striped jersey, as well as fine towelling jersey that we used for dressy soft jackets. Shoulder pads were fashionable then. When we made jackets of this type, we found that padded shoulders helped the rather flimsy jersey fabric to seem impeccably tailored.

When Cecil and the pattern cutters arrived in Belfast, there was war going on and soldiers were pointing sten guns at them (it wasn't long after Bloody Sunday). All quite scary. It was hard to imagine that the ordinary people of Belfast put up with the problems of war for so long!

Luckily those troubles seem now to have died away and Belfast is a top destination for international travellers and businessmen within Northern Ireland.

Jersey jacket

*Yellow and blue ways with the
same design*

*Mix-and-match in striped stretch jersey towelling –
this fabric had never been used before for jackets
and smart separates.*

Striped jersey tops

*Cotton jersey bustier
and skirt*

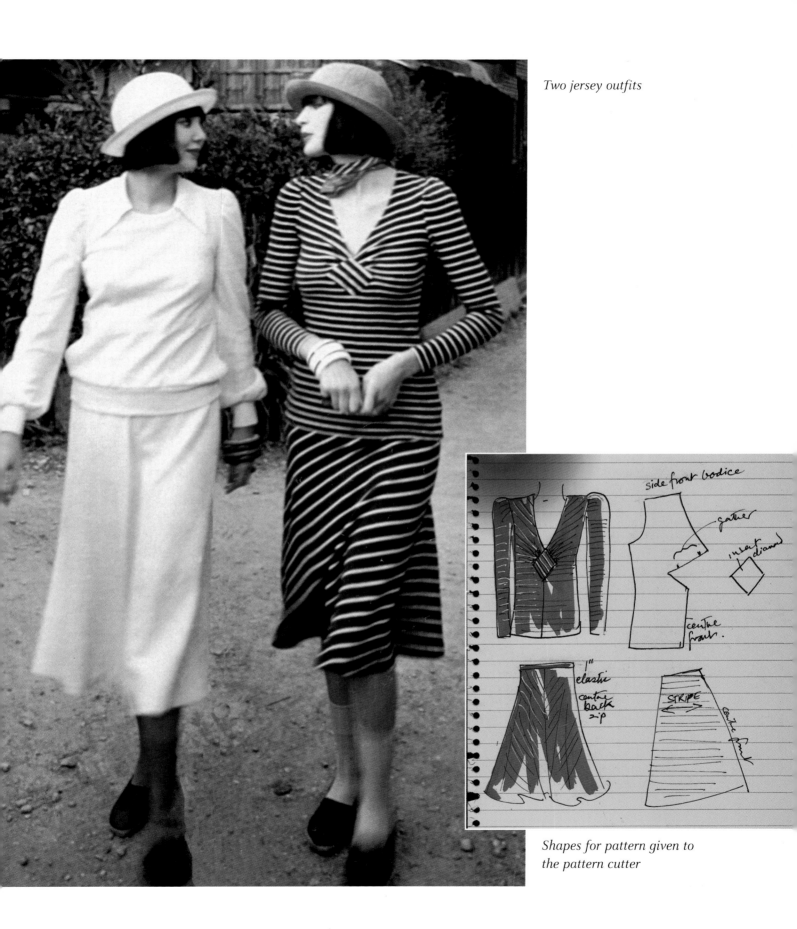

Two jersey outfits

*Shapes for pattern given to
the pattern cutter*

Chapter Four

Bus Stop and the easing of racial barriers

We all remember (at least those of us who were around) the notorious Rivers of Blood speech made by Enoch Powell in April 1968 – at the time of great campaigns for white supremacy in Britain. Many agreed with him.

Mercifully the first Race Relations Act was passed in 1968 and the mood of apartheid-style racial relations in Britain improved markedly.

Jazz musicians like Miles Davis, John Coltrane, BB King may have helped, as did Nina Simone, the Supremes and all the the Motown artists.

The Fatback Band. This American band in the 70s had a hit with a song called 'Do the Bus Stop' and decided to pose in front of Bus Stop Kensington, to have their photo taken, presumably for sending out as a publicity shot.

The original Race Relations Act, passed in 1968, showed how much Britain had learned from the anti-discrimination activities in the USA of Martin Luther King. In 1972 a new Race Relations Act was passed in Parliament. It added a so-called 'At Work' section, prohibiting employers from refusing jobs to people on the basis of their colour. Bus Stop welcomed the move wholeheartedly and made a point of catering for black girls with designs that they would find especially attractive.

Meanwhile, black power was increasingly asserting itself. The black musical *Shaft* became a box office magnet, Diana Ross played the title role in the film biography of Billie Holliday, *Lady Sings the Blues*, Bob Marley and the Wailers took over the airwaves – as did Stevie Wonder's infectious 'Superstition' and Marvin Gaye's 'I heard it through the grapevine'.

Ethnic clothes were becoming a fashion direction which would turn the whole world over. The reason was partly because the British public were beginning to holiday in much more exotic destinations: India, North Africa, the Caribbean.

Here we see the top model, charismatic Verushka, previously star of the David Hemmings' film Blow Up. *She's wearing loose-fitting Bus Stop creations which echo the robes and caftans of Egypt and Morocco.*

Bus Stop is asked to clothe the Pointer Sisters

In 1973 Bus Stop turned a new leaf in its history by bringing out *Gone with the Wind* Deep South style American outfits which the Pointer Sisters took to the moment they saw them.

Bus Stop was asked to supply some costumes for the Pointer Sisters, who were at the time touring Britain. This melodious group of stunning American black sweethearts wore them and we had publicity photographs in various publications.

They were, of course, an inventive, carousing and rhythmically driven group originally from California, who became the first girl band ever to be invited to perform at the legendary country and western Mecca known as the Grand Ole Opry in Nashville, Tennessee.

Toe-tapping, harmonious songs of real emotional draw ('Yes We Can Can', 'Wang Dang Doodle'), delivered with non-stop stage-strutting flair. Bus Stop clothes were indeed really in tune with them.

The Pointer Sisters

Chapter Five

Bus Stop and the theatrical 'Glam Rock' era

What a great time this was! All caution to the winds. Party party party! And the clothes to match! The more wild and raunchy, the better! After the subdued fashions in the years before Bus Stop, it was OK to wear the extraordinary clothes that had appeared.

Even men joined in – Skinheads and Punk Pistols as fast as they could jump on this positively post-psychedelic bandwagon!

Glamorous, androgynous David Bowie, Gothic or Heavy Metal horror rock from Black Sabbath, Guns and Roses, Metallica and Yes. Long hair for men was the norm, and this seemed to influence some of them to dress up in quite a girlie way never seen before. And Gary Glitter and Alvin Stardust, both of whom *invented* glam and spangly dresses.

The 'Swinging Sixties' were by now in the past. They marked a renaissance of free love, youthful optimism and 'can do anything' exuberance. Pop music and clothes echoed that era of heady abandon but, in the 70s, Bus Stop had to take account of a change of mood. Times were darker, with three-day weeks, industrial unrest and terrorist attacks.

People wanted to assert themselves with a whole new over-the-top lifestyle, often one of exhibitionist escapism.

In keeping with this new attitude to life, Bus Stop were now producing all kinds of outrageous, outlandish, wilder fashion statements – flared trousers, for example, and androgynous clothes showing girls dressed almost in traditional men's clothing, in jackets, ties and waistcoats.

Flamboyant, almost garish garments echoed the current trend for crazy face paint and macabre eyeliners, and the new popularity of curly beehive hair and films like *Shaft*.

Lurex zipper jacket

Lurex dress

One-shoulder dress, black-and-white satin jacquard, modelled by Kelly le Brock who later starred in The Lady in Red.

Flashy glam rock music was the universal rage – the world of Marc Bolan, the weird and wonderful Wembley Stadium antics of Queen and Freddy Mercury, and Elton John at his maddest. David Bowie, Slade, Roxy Music and Sweet. Oh, and a rather funky new band from Sweden was beginning to make waves – with the collective name of Abba.

Bus Stop catered for it all – with sequins, lurex, satins, velvets, and crazy party outfits for people wanting to 'get away from it all', and to proclaim their own semi-hallucinogenic identity.

They all met up in discos in London clubs such as Tramps, the Embassy and Maunkberry's, and in similar establishments all over the country.

It all culminated in that 1977 disco extravaganza known as *Saturday Night Fever*, with John Travolta, in pristine white suit, out-pirouetting even the great Rudolf Nureyev.

The madness and exuberance of glam rock as it used to be may have disappeared, together with the insane euphoria which accompanied it, but nowadays anything goes as far as fashion is concerned.

In 2009 the fashion crowd will mix all kinds of clothes together to create individual looks, and nothing looks unusual any more. That way they can express their individual and unique personalities.

Black wool jumpsuit with front zip

Pink and black stripe satin dress à la *Marilyn Monroe*

Marilyn Monroe (who did in fact once star in a film called *Bus Stop*!) was an eye-opener a little earlier in the 70s, but she and her style were the inspiration behind this Op Art striped dress Bus Stop brought out in 1975. Remember the scene in the Monroe film *The Seven Year Itch?* Gusts from a New York ventilation shaft blew up her dress, causing a then scandalous *billowing* effect. This image has been imitated over and over – here in *The Satin Stripe* and it still never goes out of date!

Circular skirt and lurex striped sweater

Flag brooch of diamante

Embossed velvet top and skirt,
and jumpsuit

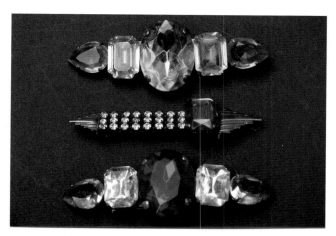

Diamante brooches

Crown brooch

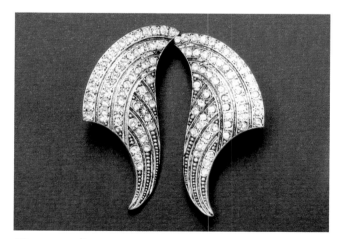

Diamante clips

Black ciré dress

The Party Era

The clothes that I designed in the 70s were, in my head, specifically made for an imaginary party girl. A girl who was out and about every night, dancing, raving, drinking and doing whatever else was around. Glam rock and sexy style became the norm.

Even day clothes, worn to the office, would lead on to going out later, having fun and looking sexy. Don't forget that all these glam rock clothes may now be commonplace. But at that time they were unavailable at the prices the average girl could afford, except at Bus Stop.

Satin top and wrap skirt

Hot pink satin zipper dress

It has to be said that when this fun period came to an end, the era that followed quite reversed the trend. Grunge was born, and in some ways it is still with us. It has influenced fashion ever since it first came in, so now it is perfectly normal to wear grungy clothes one day and to dress 'smartly' the very next.

Corkscrew earrings

Iconic Glam 70s' dress

Satin frill top photographed by David Bailey

Fun glam clothes for fun times

Party clothes included one of the most important shapes of the era – the blazer with padded shoulders, in plain and printed satins, velvets, checked and printed wools, etc.

Even the guys were wearing the Bus Stop jackets made for girls. I remember seeing Marc Bolan on TV wearing one of our silver printed black velvet jackets, and Rod Stewart wearing what looked like our white leopard printed jacket with yellow lapels.

These jackets had a touch of the Joan Crawford look about them. They were mostly worn with wide or flared trousers. Great for anyone who was a trifle big round the hips as they were cut roomily!

We made *Saturday Night Fever* blazers in white and in hot pink satin, with matching waistcoats and trousers, or short shorts worn with high boots, and three-piece suits in printed velvets and crepes.

Iconic Bus Stop jacket with leopard pattern, and satin flares

Pink satin suit

Also at this time jodhpurs had made their 'every-so-often' comeback. As they are normally worn for horse-riding, I decided to make them in khaki satin, adding a blazer jacket and a crepe frilly blouse just to add to the juxtaposition of masculine and feminine looks.

Mini-skirts and mini-dresses had also made a comeback, worn short enough to show knickers, so we really thought we were daring! Actually most women ended up wearing skirts very short – never mind their age!

Satin striped dungarees (The Sunday Times)

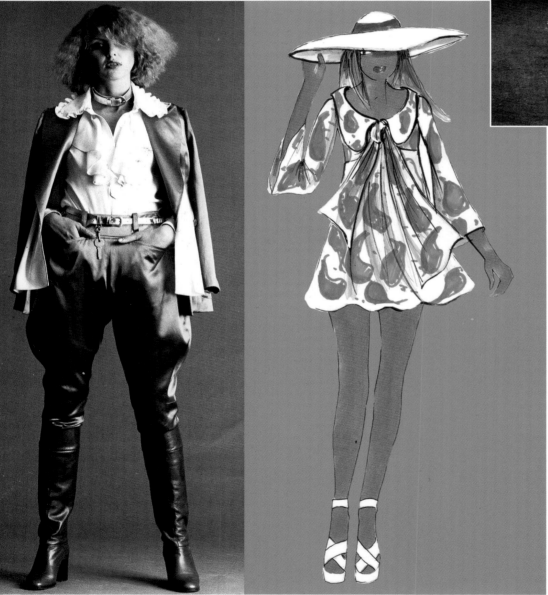

Khaki satin jodhpurs and matching jacket   *Mini dress*

It was also fun to dine out wearing satin shorts and matching blouson, which was considered quite outrageous at the time – as was our pink and black satin striped clown outfit.

A far cry from an elegant little dress!

Clown: satin baggy trousers with satin print top (The Sunday Times magazine) *– this photo has been stuck in an album ever since*

Wow! – satin shorts and blouson

White satin playsuits

We also made our own glam rock accessories: inexpensive little bags and purses made for us by artisans in feathers and matching fabrics, marvellous hats trimmed with bunches of cherries and flowers we used to order by thousands.

I found long 30s' scarves in the markets and we used them as inspiration for our own originals. Alongside we offered wonderful Bus Stop resin brooches of Marilyn Monroe, Betty Grable and other stars.

Bunch of cherries to be bought as a brooch

Bus Stop scarf

This picture appeared in a magazine in the early 70s looking very 'Chaplinesque'. The girl on the right is wearing Bus Stop clothes, navy corduroy culottes with a navy spotted blouse.

Chapter Six

Bus Stop and Fair Isle knits – and how Bus Stop turned its back on man-made fibres

Terylene, nylon and polyester began to appear in the fashion marketplace. The manufacturers of these fabrics were patting themselves on their collective backs, as these fabrics were washable and often non-iron. Unfortunately, it was then discovered that these materials cannot absorb water, so sweat cannot evaporate, causing them to be unpleasant to wear.

At the same time rayon viscose became popular. It was a fabric with a silky feel that we liked and used a lot, and is a cross between a man-made cellulose acetate and a kind of silky crepey fabric that would hang and drape well. We used it for all our prints and kept the matching plain fabric as well. It appearance certainly has the look of a natural fabric. It is also inexpensive to produce and looked a million dollars.

It is still used today, especially for T-shirts and knitwear and when knitted can be mixed with wool and cotton to give an even nicer feel. However, Bus Stop never stopped using natural cottons and wool fabrics and that was always a good selling point

One of the cultural backgrounds of the early 70s was to do with developments in industry – specifically the industry specialising in the increasing use of artificial fabrics in dress design.

Fabrics like rayon and nylon had long been a feature of manufacturers' catalogues. Such materials as Courtelle, Lycra, Terylene, Crimplene and Dacron more and more took over in the world of large-scale production.

In the mid 70s Bus Stop decided to rewrite a chapter in the history of British fashion. We wanted to bypass the world of artifice and to introduce a new generation of natural clothes in natural materials.

In other words, the traditional history of Fair Isle knits.

In the old days that's what the upper classes wore to complement their herringbone tweeds. Many girls' mums and grannies wore them as well. Bus Stop, ever anxious to herald a new trend, thought it was time to bring Fair Isle back and to turn it into more tight-fitting and feminine styles which would interest and engage the youth market of the day.

Fake fabrics were all very well, but Bus Stop's intention was to support the Fair Isle wool mills, and give their knits a new lease of life. It was good that they could continue operating in a market where man-made artificial fabrics were beginning to have too great a dominance.

One does, of course, still see girls in the street these days casually wearing shorts in the summer. But they never put together whole looks in the way we created them in the early 70s. It would be considered too 'dressed up'.

Lady knits

Fair Isle sweater with tweed midi skirt

Jersey suit with Fair Isle sweater and blouse with floppy collar

Fair Isle waistcoat with hot pants, big brimmed hat, bangles, coloured tights, puff-sleeved blouse, ankle-strapped wedges

There is never anything totally new in fashion. The cycle goes round and fashion always returns in a slightly different form.

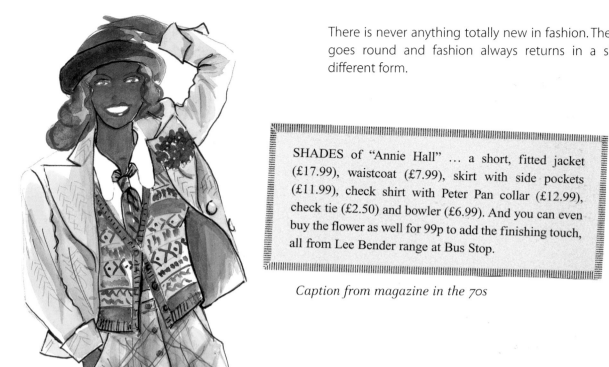

Annie Hall suit

SHADES of "Annie Hall" … a short, fitted jacket (£17.99), waistcoat (£7.99), skirt with side pockets (£11.99), check shirt with Peter Pan collar (£12.99), check tie (£2.50) and bowler (£6.99). And you can even buy the flower as well for 99p to add the finishing touch, all from Lee Bender range at Bus Stop.

Caption from magazine in the 70s

Fair Isle cardigan with matching print blouse and cap in same colours

Mickey brooch

Chapter Seven

Bus Stop: informality and beachwear

The mood had become informal, innovative, experimental and far-out, just in the way society had by now become during the Bus Stop era.

It was no longer essential to dress up and wear cocktail gowns, ballgowns, black tie, white tie. Dressed-up uniforms of earlier decades had now been put back in the wardrobe or the Louis Vuitton trunk.

You could wear whatever you pleased, all mixed up – and whichever way it all suited you best

By the mid 70s, a new style of living had become the norm in Britain. Fashion seekers had more clothing alternatives to choose from than at any other time in history. Living became much more informal than it had been in the old days, and girls and women had developed lifestyles of unparalleled width and variety.

In the old days, husbands had most often supported their wives, who stayed at home and looked after the children. But in the mid 70s women (and girls!) were suddenly offered jobs which had been the birthright only of men. Women went to business meetings. They had office occasions to attend, from lunches to conferences.

It simply wasn't any longer necessary to dress as formally as in the pre-Bus Stop days, and at Bus Stop we made sure that we could offer our shoppers much more casual clothing for all the new lifestyles.

All-in-one swimsuit

Blue-and-white
jersey bikini

People had more leisure time on their hands. More chance to buy cheap country houses and renovate them. More ability to afford exotic holidays in sunny climes abroad. So one of Bus Stop's new areas of emphasis was the world of cheap but very cheerful swimwear and certain beachwear that could be worn in the street.

Barbara Bach in the Viva Maria outfit (printed across the centrefold of The Sunday Times *magazine)*

Bus Stop created all kinds of alluring swimsuits

From a glamorous, star-studded Rita Hayworth one-piece, to daring, stunning bikinis straight out of the Club 55 in St Tropez (still going strong today!)

From swimsuits printed with balmy scenes straight out of tropical Hawaii – aloha!

From designs in blue and yellow showing the sun and Mediterranean skies

From prints with castanets and Spanish guitars to bikinis in alluring flesh tones – so you hardly knew whether the bikini was bikini, or plain naked skin.

We made a small run of this fruity swimsuit in a jersey that had some lycra woven into it. I couldn't resist adding a drawing of a bowl of fruit upon the model's head!

Stripey jersey beach dress

Barbara Bach modelling a striped and lace-trimmed seersucker top with shorts for The Sunday Times *magazine*

Playsuits in spots and stripes: illustrated are Bus Stop's little playsuits. A kind of short jumpsuit you could wear on the beach – and also for going out to dinner and discos.

Hot pants and shorts became the holiday standard. You could wear shorts during the warm summer days and a maxi dress the next day to add to the surprise effect.

White shorts and stripey top

White satin shorts with appliqué work and matching elasticised bandeau (from the Daily Record*)*

Shorts and shirt, plus coolie hat (This was termed an 'After Disco outfit' by the Daily Record*.)*

Dotty playsuit

Lurex bikinis: very daring Bus Stop lurex bikinis and shorts!

Jersey fabric three-piece playsuit

Cotton sunsuit

Bikini and wrap skirt

Bus Stop boiler suits in two long hot summers

Remember the terrifying floods which nearly drowned the lovely Cornish village of Boscastle in 2004? Remember the soaking, dire summers of 2007 and 2008, with more floods all over Britain, endless grey skies and diabolical Augusts and Septembers – the worst on record?

It's time to look upon the 'sunny side of the street', even if that does mean harking back to the two amazing summers of 1975 and 1976, when the sun, cloudlessness, the heat and the ice-cream consumption reminded contemporary observers of typical summer weather in downtown Athens.

Long Hot Summer

What this all meant were virtually unbroken months of 90° temperatures. Well, 'some liked it hot' and others didn't.

We've seen how all kinds of external factors influenced what was in the Bus Stop stores throughout the 70s. These included developments in the arts, in music, in racial harmony, in films, in politics and in new trends for clubs and parties. The major decisive element for Bus Stop during the two years of 1975 and 1976 was something very different. In short, the astonishing, unexpected and boiling English weather.

Bus Stop responded by bringing out a new collection of jumpsuits which we preferred to call *boiler suits*. They consisted of dresses which had somehow sprouted trousers where the dress hem would normally have been. They were in fact a little like a kind of feminine trouser garment. They did, of course, offer a good deal of protection against the sun's determination to tan and burn the legs. Which – if you'll forgive – is why Bus Stop boiler suits started selling like a house on fire.

Cotton jumpsuit

Dressy jumpsuit

Red check and spot jumpsuit

LEE BENDER
AUTUMN '76

BEACHWEAR 63

Striped seersucker dungarees

Dupion dungarees

Zip boiler suit

White drawstring neck jumpsuit in cheesecloth

Drawstring jacket and sheath dress

Seersucker wool tartan shorts and blazer, worn with shirt and short-sleeved sweater

Chapter Eight

Bus Stop and Scottish tartan

Tartan is an ornament which, whatever the history, is strongly associated with the proud fiefdom world of Macbeth, Macduff, the Bruces – and all the rugged Bravehearts of the chequered story of Scotland. It was a favourite of Queen Victoria who not only dressed flamboyantly in tartan velvet but dressed all her nine children in it also. Balmoral in 1858 was decked out in tartan. It is worn today by the Royal Family when they are in Scotland, especially by the Queen.

Kilts, capes, coats, skirts, sweaters in tartan are discovered over and over again, as are tartan rugs, tablecloths, table napkins and often wallpaper.

In 2008 tartan once again made a comeback. As this fashion can be a 'flash-in-the-pan', manufacturers have to be really careful to get the timing right when launching a tartan collection. Bring it in too soon and it won't sell. Bring it in too late and the manufacturer will get stuck with it. Tartan will then be relegated back to Scottish souvenir shops and traditionalism, only to be worn by Scottish grannies, and at Scottish balls and Highland reels.

Tartans were developed through the Middle Ages, and particularly in the seventeenth century at the time of powerful Scottish clans. After the Jacobite Rebellion of 1745, when Bonnie Prince Charlie tried to restore the Stuarts to the British throne, the wearing of tartan was outlawed – to be legalised again in 1782.

In about 1974 the idea of tartan kilts with traditional Shetland sweaters had become the rage in France. Britain was being invaded by French girls who hurried to specialist little Scottish shops in London to buy kilts and sweaters in children's sizes, because they preferred tight-fitting clothes! Tartan then being woven was in traditional clan colours and also in such colours as natural pinks, blues, beiges and greens.

Tartan swatches

All this inspired me to design a line of mini-kilts and small Shetland sweaters, to be made in materials already dyed in bright colours for Bus Stop.

*Kilts with matching
Shetland sweaters*

Sketch of a jumpsuit trimmed with tartan, given to the pattern cutter

Checked waistcoats and rolled-up trousers

Yellow tartan

Velvet co-ordinates: red-edged velvet jacket, velvet skirt, wool tartan waistcoat, tartan and patent bag, matching tartan hat and scarf, velvet fitted dress, tartan boots, tartan gloves

Twin tartan outfits

Feeding the dog

Hi, from the Highlands of Scotland

The success of the Shetland sweaters among the French teenagers led me to research and develop a whole new outlook on what could be made of the Scottish Connection. Tartans had, so to speak, always been with us and it seemed to Bus Stop that they could indeed become a new craze for the mid 70s.

The palace of Holyroodhouse

Just look at what was going on in Scotland: the Edinburgh Festival was by now one of the premier cultural events of the United Kingdom; single malt whisky was fast becoming one of the most palatable drinking experiences; kilts were back in fashion; the Loch Ness monster, after several 'sightings', was rearing its ugly head again.

Haggis for breakfast had taken on a new attraction. Rod Stewart was fast becoming one of the most popular British – sorry, Scottish – singers ever. Following behind him were the Bay City Rollers, and the group Slade who, though hailing from Wolverhampton, always seemed to be sporting Scottish tartans.

In the mid 70s all things Scottish were a centre of attention. Scotland was no longer viewed just as a land of aristocratic and exclusive grouse shooting, golf courses for nonagenarians, dour Highland scenery and incessant rain – but a land of strength and inspiration.

So Bus Stop went full throttle Tartan! With tartan kilts, high-shouldered jackets and suits complete with Scottish fully pocketed waistcoats, and fully flared new Scottish overcoats in the new bright tartan colours. All this accompanied by tartan skirts, hats, bags, tights, the whole caboodle of moods and modes of the moment.

Plaid wool flared coat

Long wool tartan skirt

Tartan check jacket and black shorts

Yellow waistcoat and trousers, with jacket and skirt above

In the 70s before Bus Stop entered the fray, designers had always used tartan patterns on woollen fabrics, often used as the lining of traditional overcoats where they couldn't be seen. It was time to put new thinking into what could be done with this potentially versatile material.

Here we see one of Bus Stop's new breakthroughs. It's a tartan raincoat, with the tartan design incorporated into waterproof gaberdine. Nobody until now had made a success from such an experiment.

Three-piece trouser suit in red and khaki wool, enlarged Prince of Wales check

Checked gaberdine raincoat

Chapter Nine

Bus Stop and tea dresses

The definition of a tea dress:

A tea-gown was a woman's at home dress from the late nineteenth to the mid twentieth centuries characterised by light and printed fabrics.

In contemporary usage, any flowing dress of sheer or translucent fabric in mainly pastel colours, mid calf to ankle length may be called a tea gown.

One does not go out to dine in a tea-gown except in the house of a member of one's family or a most intimate friend. One would wear a tea-gown in one's own house in receiving a guest to whose house one would wear a dinner dress.

Emily Post, *Etiquette*, 1922

In the midst of all the modernistic influences of the mid 70s, one somewhat contradictory emotional attachment always remained. To put it at is most simple, NOSTALGIA, a hankering for the simpler, more graceful lives and values always associated with the generations of the 20s and 30s.

I've said before that 'there is never anything totally new in fashion'. It always returns again and again in a slightly different form.

Look at the number of girls today who visit all kinds of vintage clothes stores looking for evening-type lacy garments which can be worn as daywear. These are usually tops or dresses reminiscent of the early 30s, with fine lace filigree, and exquisite cut and detail. Markets all over London, Britain, Paris and the Continent do a roaring trade in such heritage garments, which don't seem to have dated at all!

The same curiosity drove girls and women in the 70s. When the Redford and Streisand film, *The Great Gatsby*, came out in 1974, there was a wondrous revival of interest in the fashions its stars were able to re-create.

Bus Stop decided – as another episode in its ever-changing history – to explore the vintage look in detail, using markets as reference points for clothes which would re-create today the courteous and unhurried atmosphere of an earlier age.

Before the Second World War, the ubiquitous tea dress was a highly popular choice for wearing not only at teatime, but at lunch and at dinner. And Elsa Schiaparelli, the famous couturier, was known for her soft, satin and crepe flowery dresses which exuded a body-hugging svelte allure. Any woman wearing one of her creations – the moment she began walking – would be the cynosure of all eyes.

*Viscose printed crepe top
and skirt with frilled top
and wrap-over skirt*

Back view of frill

Printed crepe de chine tea dress

Floral two-piece with matching scarf

FOUR DRESSY TOPS
1. *Printed crepe blouse, pointed collar*
2. *Satin top*
3. *Printed crepe top wiith music notes*
4. *Grey and red spot top*

Bus Stop tea dresses were usually made in dreamy watery printed soft crepes and satins, often cut on the bias, which clung to the body and accentuated the best bits of the wearer.

The point was that they had a quality of quiet elegance and sexiness, quite different from the way-out impressions other Bus Stop outfits created. They could also be worn everywhere, to the office, out to tea, to drinks, to dinner, to parties – anywhere.

From a designer's point of view, a garment which has multiple versatility is a sure-fire bestseller. Much better than an everyday something-or-other just to go out shopping or wear around the house. After all, we females don't mind parting with our hard-earned cash if we can wear the garment to death all over the place and look wonderful in it at all times!

Four dressy satin bottoms to match

Floral two-piece photo

Silky duo

Here are two girls in 1975 showing off their Bus Stop tea dresses

Crepe de chine swatch

Bus Stop dresses

Black print dress

*Flowered jersey dress –
cherries pinned onto hat*

White print jersey dress

TEA DRESSES

Red crepe dress

Red embossed velvet with matching fringed scarf

Red beret with purple dress

How long did it take to produce this crepe tea dress?

From adapting a print design found in an antique market, discussing it with the designer from the fabric company and getting the samples made	3 weeks
To confirm, cost, price and order fabric	6 weeks
To design and make the style	2 weeks
To send samples to the factory for a copy and then check in the sample room	2 weeks
To grade the patterns into sizes	2 weeks
To send the fabric to the factory and produce the stock	4 weeks
Total time to produce the fabric and make our own print garment	**4 months**

This was a working tea dress drawing given to the pattern cutters which I oversaw. Sometimes I would make an important part of the pattern myself, so that I could be sure that the garment had the right look. The interpretation is key when working with a cutter, as it is necessary to get the shape required for the garment.

We would all like to wear this now! The little printed crepe tea dress of 1971 cost just £7.50.

40s' look tea dresses

A little different from the 30s' style. But I used to love designing both. The 40s' version featured padded shoulders to achieve the right silhouette. In the case of these two dresses, we often produced the same garment in various different fabrics. This was the advantage of owning shops – you get to make the rules!

Tea dresses in jersey prints

Tea dresses, a revival of the glamorous earlier versions of the 30s, became a very serious seller in the Bus Stop 70s' overall story!

The fabric used here is a crepe print that was designed exclusively for Bus Stop. We originally found it in a vintage shop and adapted the print to fit in with the printing works' abilities.

When using fabric exclusive to Bus Stop, we had to order fairly large quantities, to make it possible for the printer to keep it for us and not to allow others to buy the same print. It was therefore necessary to design a variety of different styles in order to use the required quantity of fabric. It proved to be a good idea anyway, as it allowed the shopper to mix and match the garments.

White printed crepe dress

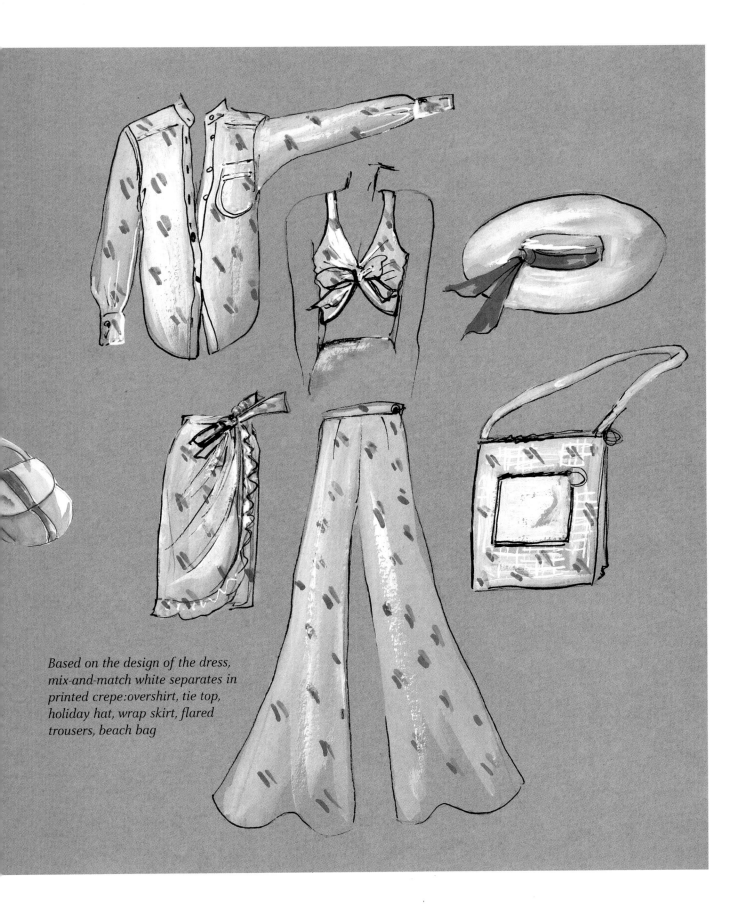

Based on the design of the dress,
mix-and-match white separates in
printed crepe:overshirt, tie top,
holiday hat, wrap skirt, flared
trousers, beach bag

The Vintage Look

It's a funny old term, VINTAGE. It is frequently applied to early twentieth-century motor cars and to mature port.

In good times when every type of fashion look had been around, many girls wanted to return to antique clothing, as a reaction against all the others. Returning to the more whimsical and, in a way, more individual looks of vintage fashion was the only option. It followed that tea dresses, tops and blouses, often in tiny flowered prints and lace appliqué fitted in perfectly with the vintage look. In fact, vintage clothing has never gone out of fashion.

I found this vintage top in 1973 and it was probably made in the 40s. We subsequently made a similar garment to be worn with jeans.

Six ways with crepe and lace

Vintage look as seen today

If I were designing for Bus Stop today, the top would have inspired these dresses.

Hailing the bus

Chapter Ten

Bus Stop and the Op Art movement

The worlds of art and fashion have always acted as mirror images of each other.

Look at the work of the Dutch painter Mondrian, who died in New York in 1944. He was long famous for his paintings in geometrical coloured squares and rectangles in different shades – grey, blue, white, red, yellow, etc. His body of work formed the basis of the 60s' styles of Courrèges, whose outfits reminded many of Mondrian's painting.

Look at the T-shirt industry, with its designs often echoing the French Impressionists, Picasso, Chagall, Miró and a myriad of well-known names from painting.

Recently jeans were on sale in London with a glittering encrusted Technicolor replica of the famous artist Damien Hirst's diamond skull sewn onto the back pocket. Fashion imitating art summed up this remarkable garment.

In the mid 70s, Op Art was the centre of attention. Its dizzying, disorientating effects, with Bridget Riley its most prominent partisan, helped influence the new collections at Bus Stop at that time.

Op Art

One of its originators was the Hungarian, Victor Vasarely, who twisted visual effects in shimmering and scintillating distortions.

Shapes, patterns, optical illusions – many in black and white – were experimented with in mind-boggling ways. Op Art made paintings seem to move as your eyes grew accustomed to them. In fact the movement had another name derived from movement – Kinetic Art.

Graphic designers had experimented with Op Art before, notably Yves Saint Laurent and Courrèges. But Op Art fashion had never really entered the mass market consciousness, which is why, in the mid 70s, I wanted to explore these optical motifs in fashion.

Spots, matching checks and stripes were my favourites

I found that Op Art's graphic dimension allowed Bus Stop to present fashion in its most 'showy' way.

Girls who want to be noticed were my audience. Not in a flamboyant, sexy way, but in a well-dressed artistically aware kind of manner. That was what this aspect of the Bus Stop 70s' story was all about. Op Art also stood for perfect and fun business dressing.

Tights package – tights which matched the clothes in colour

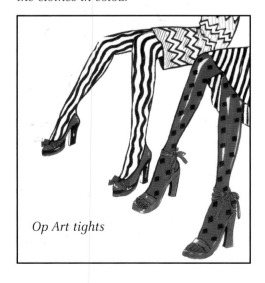

Op Art tights

Spots, checks...

...and stripes

Striped blouse

Zigzag knit coat

Black/white Op Art Bus Stop scarf

Triangle brooch

Zigzag sweater

Striped shirt dress

Bouclé striped sweater

Jersey three-piece

Halter neck jumpsuit with striped jersey cardigan, made of puppy-tooth tweed and striped jersey

Black and white checks, Op Art style

The line check and puppy-tooth contrast that we used for the jumpsuits and boiler suits made a perfect team with the cotton-mix black and white striped jersey for the cardigan.

These were worn casually in a 30s' style and were made in all colours. In the shop display we teamed the checks with a 30s' black and white scarf, also for sale.

Checked jumpsuit, made of checked linen and spotted black polyester

Checked Harris tweed had been a mainline material in both men's and women's fashion since time immemorial. By the mid 70s, however, the 'tweed and twill' self-projection was seen as a little 'old fashioned and country house'.

Bus Stop's purpose here was to pay homage to the family weavers in the Hebrides, whose livelihood to some extent depended on support from clothes retailers on the UK mainland.

Checks and stripes were printed on 'linen-look' rayon to give an unexpected Op Art version of traditional tweed patterns.

Striped and checked suits in 'linen-look'

Other styles we made in the check fabrics

Shirtwaist dress

Black and white checked linen: tailored jacket (with a spotted red blouse), straight skirt with side split, long skirt cut on cross, hat made up in check fabric to match the clothes (flowers were sold separately). We made this outfit in lots of different checked fabrics.

Fabric No. 8

Viscose swing jacket and elasticised tank top in cream with large red spots + swatches

Mix-and-match was what the 70s were all about. As long as the fabrics and colours matched, one could wear a mini skirt one day, a maxi dress or trousers the next day or hot pants the day after. That's what women did. Trousers and trouser suits were serious fashion as well as practical.

Even in those days, the outfit below was considered really inexpensive. As the girls rushed in on a Saturday to buy new clothes, they found that it was not necessary to buy the whole outfit at once, but just to keep adding to it week after week.

The Bus Stop look, October 1975

These were the prices in October 1975

Black spotted cream blouse	£6.95
Reverse colour crepe cardigan	£5.95
White crepe trousers	£5.95
Patent belt	£2.50
Black felt hat	£2.95
Total	**£24.30**

MINK

CHINCHILLA

ERMINE

LEOPARD

OCELOT

SEALSKIN

FOX

JAGUAR

Etc.

Chapter Eleven

Bus Stop and fake fur

The mass murder of innocent animals for fur began to cause a widespread new public revulsion and we at Bus Stop were certainly aware of it.

In the days of early twentieth-century Hollywood, it was, of course, the fashionable thing at film premieres to emerge from your Cadillac or Bentley wrapped in a mink coat or a chinchilla cape and diamonds. You then presented yourself to a adoring public amidst flashlights and universal acclaim, especially if you were Rita Hayworth or Marilyn Monroe, Grace Kelly or Ava Gardner.

Exotic furs were all the rage until the 70s – Hollywood stars in ermine stoles, etc. – and were worn religiously by the monied classes, mostly to show off their wealth, rather than to protect themselves against the cold.

We were completely opposed to the commercial hunting of new-born animals such as seals, otter, mink, etc. To us it represented cruelty at its extreme, and we'd got a far more humane idea …

Fake fur!

Around that time Animal Rights movements were raising public protest over the number of animals facing extinction. Such protest was publicised round the world and created near riots whenever wearers of non-PC furs were spotted flaunting their valuable possessions.

Bus Stop had a much better slant on the problem:

What about making fur that wasn't fur but used materials which looked like it?

Fake fur beaver tie-belted jacket

Fun, spoof fur coats made out of fake fur materials. Imaginatively cut, dyed, mixed with suede and leather, and styled in imaginative new designs. Owners could enjoy the cachet of a fur coat but without having to feel the guilt of slaughtering a real animal to do so!

Fake leopard-skin jacket (price £39.99 in the 70s)

Anti-fur group gets all catty

Rome, 16 August 2008
The Animal Rights Movement is still very much with us!

Recently 2000 signatures were delivered to the Vatican asking the Pope to stop wearing papal garments still trimmed with ermine. It is believed that Pope Benedict has already given up his official fur-trimmed hat and cloak. And what about the bearskin hats still worn by the Guards?

Bus Stop fake lambskin coat shown in Vogue

White teddybear trench coat (price £39.99 in the 70s)

Ginger curly furry Borg jigger coat (price £14.95), with stitched green cloche hat, yellow striped polo neck sweater (price £3.95) and sawn-off green Oxford bags (£5.95)

Chapter Twelve

Bus Stop and the military look

It has been said that fashion is influenced by world events such as wars. As there are wars at any given time in various parts of the world, it should follow that military fashion is always in. But the mere nature of fashion is such a fast-changing business that moving on to other looks becomes a necessity.

The military look, being boyish and androgynous, can look wonderful and sexy on a feminine female. That is the whole point of girls wearing this look. It is the shock mixture of feminine and masculine together that is attractive.

Think of the armour and leggings of the Roman army, of the bare-breasted warlike style of the English warrior queen Boadicea who fought the Romans in the first century AD, and of Joan of Arc, in white armour with her own emblem, resisting the English troops in Orléans in 1429.

1975 saw another unfolding episode in Bus Stop history, this time influenced by the activities of armed forces. In that year the US army and embassy staff were expelled from the Vietnamese capital of Saigon – since renamed Ho Chi Minh City – and that long-lasting war was over.

Quite often during war in various world arenas, fashion is influenced by martial considerations. And surges of military styles are put on the market in the usual colours of khaki, navy and Air Force blue.

On this occasion Bus Stop was part of the vanguard of the new 'uniform fashion' all over Britain. We produced all kinds of styles: trousers with multi-pockets, tunics, brass buttons, combat jackets, caps, heavy leather belts and various pieces of military baggage. I designed military jumpsuits with both shorts and long trousers, wrap-round dresses (army style) in various lengths, sweaters with épaulettes, bags and scarves.

Military jumpsuit with striped sweater

Converse boots

Military paraphernalia

Khaki sequin cap

Midi dress

123

6952

732

660

208

Camouflage fabric was an automatic favourite for the clothing industry in this market, making collections reminiscent of full military dress. However, we at Bus Stop left camouflage well alone, because everyone else was on that bandwagon and we always wanted to be different.

Wrap dress with set of matching shawl, sweater and leggings

Khaki separates and accessories: ribbed one-shoulder top, ribbed top, jacket with zips, wrap skirt, long skirt – midi with fly front, browny leather bag and chain, camouflage purse, waistcoat, belt with chain, camouflage cap and polo, ribbed scarf

Sheriff star badge

Big lizard

Sheriff badges

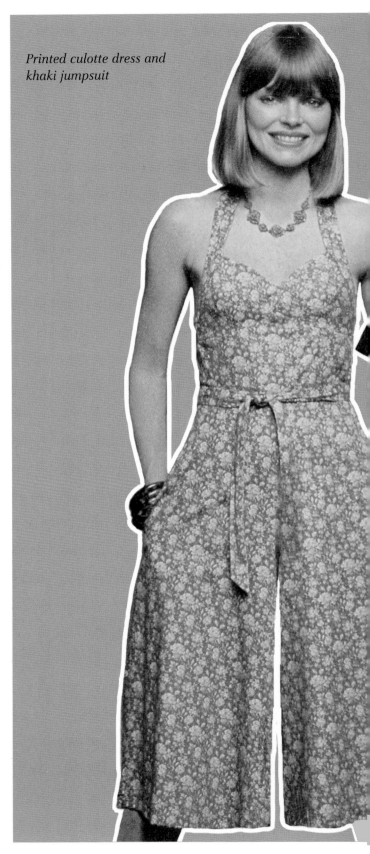

Printed culotte dress and khaki jumpsuit

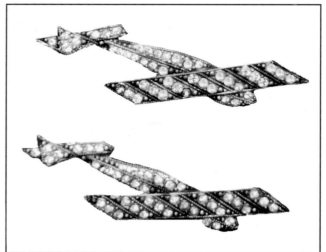

Aeroplane brooches

*Khaki jumpsuit
with short trousers*

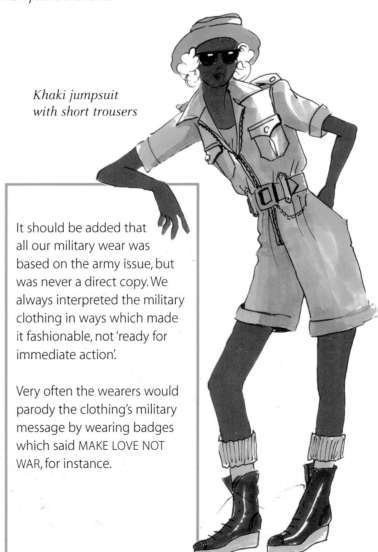

It should be added that all our military wear was based on the army issue, but was never a direct copy. We always interpreted the military clothing in ways which made it fashionable, not 'ready for immediate action'.

Very often the wearers would parody the clothing's military message by wearing badges which said MAKE LOVE NOT WAR, for instance.

Chapter Thirteen

Bus Stop and an Aladdin's Cave of accessories and jewellery

Accessories are a fun way of dressing up our wardrobes. When money is tight, all we need do is to buy a new scarf, or new shoes, or a new sweater, or a piece of costume jewellery to cheer ourselves up, and transform the clothes and our look.

In fact that is the way to make the garment that you have bought different from that of the next person, just by changing the accessories. From the shopkeeper's point of view, it is very welcome revenue in addition to what has been paid by the customer for her major purchase.

All through the decade of Bus Stop's existence, the shops became havens of fantastic additional touches which went along with the clothes on offer each season. Very often, our accessories and jewellery were designed to match the mood of the collections we were then offering. Whenever you came in, you'd find a brand new selection of extra goodies of the moment.

The idea, of course, was to extend Bus Stop's purpose by turning it into a mini-department store. It meant that we could dress girls in our fashions from head to foot. Proper top-to-toe co-ordination!

We sold hats, bags, scarves, purses, wallets, feathers and feather boas, flower trimmings, flower bouquets, tights, leggings, gloves, shoes, boots and underwear, all to match our clothes in the colours of the moment – and complementary to their innate design. We even sold beautiful satin and lace underwear and jersey bikinis with little overskirts.

Parrot brooch

Buying, or designing and making, these appetising little extras was simply endless fun – fun we tried to make sure our customers enjoyed just the way we did!

Knitted 'pillbox' and scarf

Green hat

Knitted hat

Red pillbox

Pink laced boots

Platform-heeled sandals

Knitted sweater

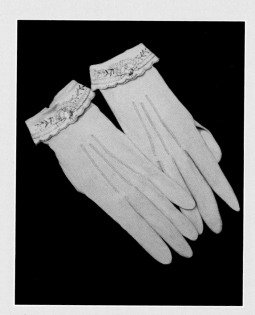

Gloves

Spotty wedges

As for jewellery, Bus Stop was like a Kensington version of *Breakfast at Tiffany's* – but at a much more sensible price!

Over that period we managed to buy or design practically everything money could buy – and not too much money at that!

★ brooches in magnificent Art Deco settings

★ chunky bracelets to wear round the wrist

★ official-looking Arizona Sheriff badges to decorate any cowboy style of shirt

★ necklaces of all shapes, designs and sizes

★ the world's most fetching earrings straight out of *La Dolce Vita* and its successors

★ Pop Art Andy Warhol medals featuring such cultural heroes as Marilyn Monroe and the healthy, heartening Campbell Tomato Soup can

Many of these 'objets d'art' still command simply extortionate prices!

Lizard brooch

The steel and resin pieces illustrated here belonged to a jewellery maker from Paris who went bankrupt. We bought up some of the bankruptcy stock. I have managed to keep the few pieces for all these years, even though I could have sold them many times over.

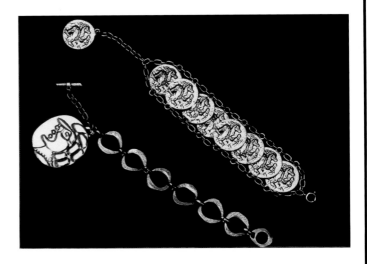

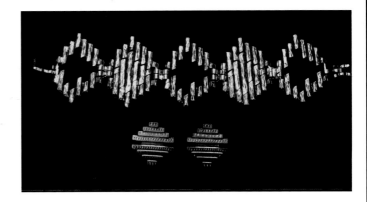

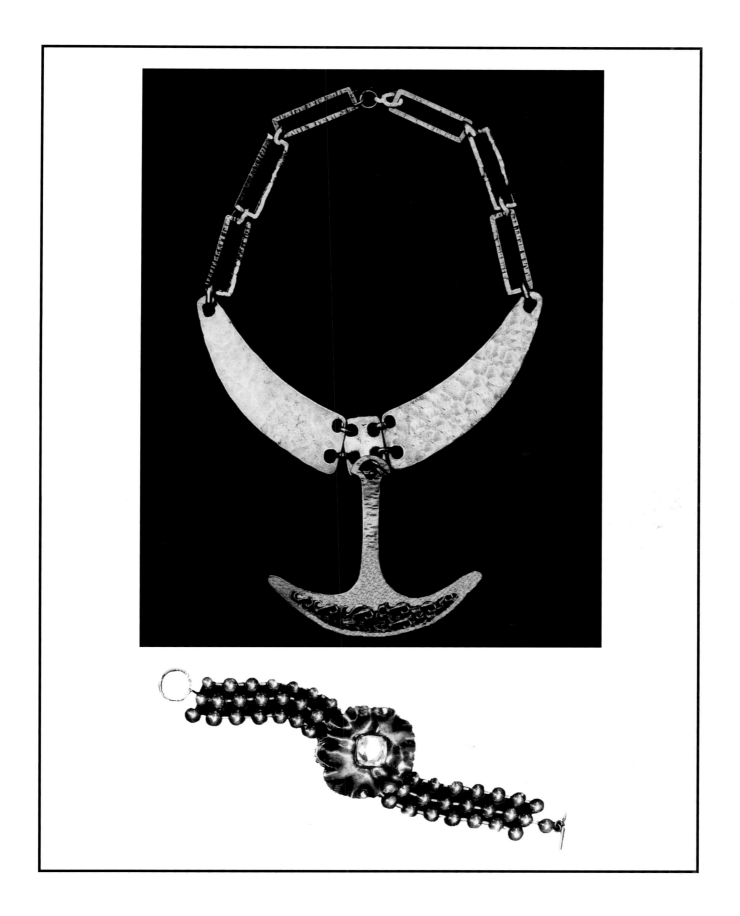

Statue of Liberty

Chapter Fourteen

Bus Stop and globalisation

Globalisation.

A favourite piece of catchword jargon in the business and cultural worlds of the early twenty-first century. And look what has just happened: Tesco and Boots have stores all over Thailand.

Illustrious names such as Hermès, Dior, Gucci, Chanel, are to be found not only in Paris, but also in Beijing, Shanghai, Rio, Dubai, and anywhere where there are people with big money.

And look at Body Shop: a company which began with a simple hunch during Anita Roddick's early days in Brighton. And now there are Body Shops literally all over the world.

'THE WORLD IS A GLOBAL VILLAGE', said Marshall McLuhan in 1967, and successful interpreters of this philosophy have broadened their commercial vision to dimensions far beyond any ordinary expectation.

Bus Stop cannot claim ever to have rivalled the inordinate worldwide go-getting of such companies as those mentioned. BUT WE CERTAINLY DID EXPAND BEYOND THESE SHORES AND WITH GREAT SUCCESS.

When we opened the second Bus Stop shop in Glasgow, we were surprised and delighted to find that we had the same queues and crowds as in London. Indeed, Glasgow sales turned out to be just as booming as they were in London. And Glasgow girls fell for the Bus Stop styles in exactly the same enthusiastic way. So we started up in Edinburgh – with what was to become another of our most money-spinning stores.

Liverpool followed. And Newcastle. And Leeds. And Manchester, Birmingham, Nottingham, Southampton, Bristol and Brighton.

All the shop staff had been specially chosen for their looks and figures – and they had to wear Bus Stop clothes as uniform. They were so excited about the clothes that they put on fashion shows, often in a local club – or even in the shops – using themselves as models. Bus Stop salesgirls thus showed our top-to-toe co-ordination in action.

We really wanted to see if Bus Stop's philosophy worked countrywide. And it did. Bus Stop remained alive and well long after the earliest UK boutiques of its era had waned and faded.

Every Saturday Cecil would telephone each boutique to see how sales were going. And every season Bus Stop salesgirls came down to London to see what the latest styles were going to look like – well in advance.

Expansion took place both in the UK and – as we shall soon see – all over the world!

Bus Stop expansion in the UK by 1979

The twelve shops added up to a network bringing Bus Stop styles all over Britain.

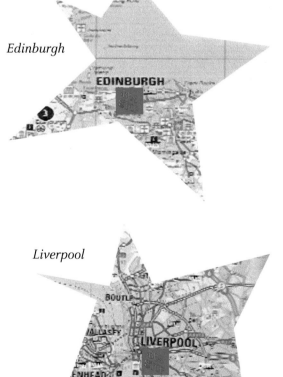

The original Bus Stop shop in London

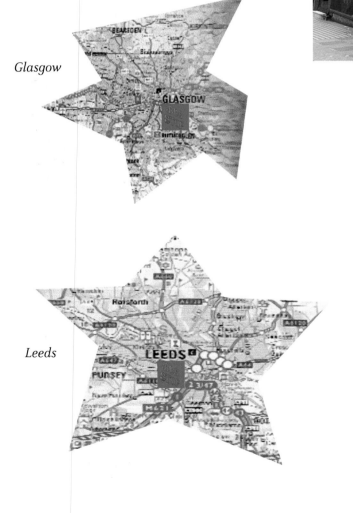

Glasgow

Edinburgh

Leeds

Liverpool

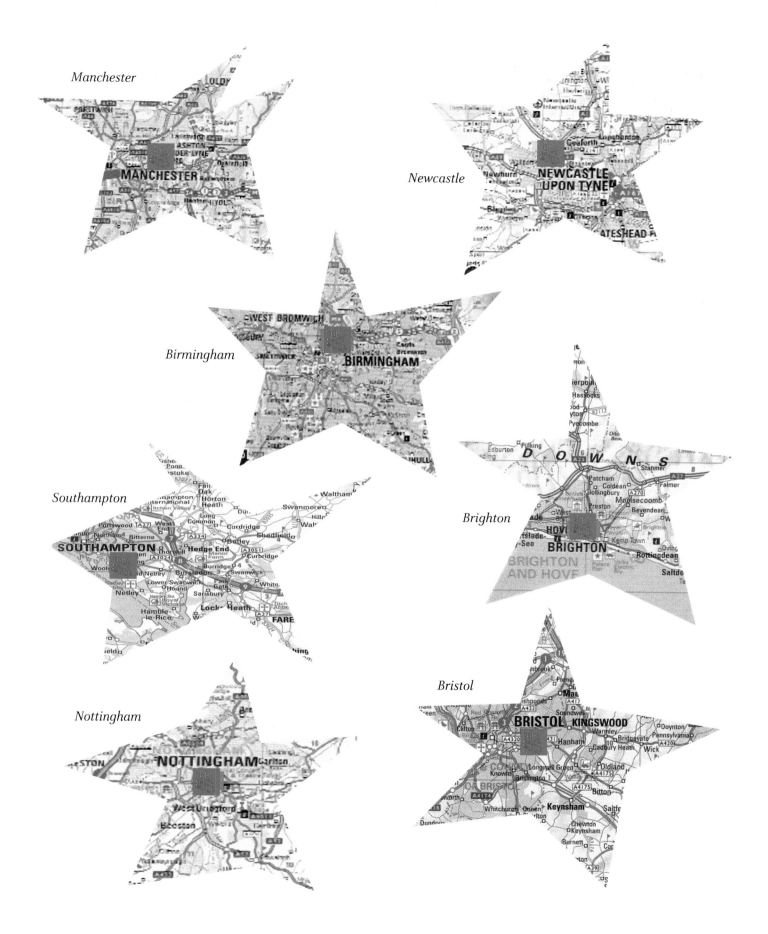

'New York, New York – it's a wonderful town!'

In the closing years of the 70s, Bus Stop's expansion in the UK began to point to an enlargement of the Bus Stop boundaries. And so Cecil and I decided

America, here we come!

Early in August 1978, Bus Stop opened a shop in Bloomingdale's, New York (600 sq. ft.) in Hudson's in Detroit and Cleveland, Ohio, and Carlson Pirie Scott in Chicago. In September of the same year, similar boutiques opened in Bloomingdale's in Boston and in Hutchinson's in Hong Kong.

The Bloomingdale fashion direction executives had been following Bus Stop's UK progress for most of the decade. 'Lee Bender,' they wrote, 'is in the forefront of international fashion. She has *the* looks from London, Paris and Milan. One of the most exciting aspects is her use of colour.'

Bus Stop at Bloomingdale's, a semi-replica of Kensington Church Street, was put together on a raised platform. I featured the same red-lacquered walls as in the original London shop and interior design with the same atmosphere.

HALF THE STOCK WAS SOLD IN ONE AMAZINGLY SHORT WEEK!

And Bus Stop's glamorous slippery satin pyjama suits at once became New York's favourite evening look.

question: how far is it from buckingham palace to bloomingdale's? answer: just one bus stop ...
it's an express ... direct from london ... and here in the 13 colonies, it's ours alone!

Introducing Bus Stop at Bloomingdale's, the shop countless British girls wouldn't get dressed without. Now you don't have to either. Because we've re-created it all right here. It's our brand-new, lacquered-up, bright red British Boutique, that divides your dressing into three dimensions: Black/White ... Night ... and Day. And if this kind of excitement makes you want to meet the Londoner who designed and started it all—you can. Lee Bender will be here today to christen our rendition of her shop. Come see why body English will never be the same. Bus Stop, Plaza 2 Juniors, Second Floor.

A sample in silhouettes. The B&W of it: padded jacket, wool pant and vest, and a T that says Bus Stop right there/The Night of it: satiny smoking jacket, camisole and pants/The Day of it: tweed blazer, plaid vest and skirt, and button down shirt/ And we've a collectionful: jackets from 55.00 to 86.00; skirts from 36.00 to 50.00; blouses from 28.00 to 44.00; and trousers from 46.00 to 60.00.

Meet Lee and Cecil Bender, the prime movers, today from noon to two when there'll be informal modeling in Bus Stop, Second Floor, New York.

bloomingdale's

it's like no other store in the world

Bloomingdale's poster

Poster for the Carlson Pirie Scott store in Chicago

Later Bus Stop held fashion shows by the dozen in The Bay, Montreal, Canada. Bus Stop's influence in the States started to repeat the dynamic growth pattern earlier experienced all over the UK.

Montreal Gazette

1978 onwards – Bus Stop explores new frontiers in Europe and the Far East

At a later stage in the Bus Stop UK expansion, we decided to make a sortie into Continental Europe.

Bus Stop, Amsterdam, did in fact open a little earlier, in 1976 – a new landmark in that atmospheric city of canals, tulips, salt herring snacks, Rembrandt and Vermeer. Dutch girls loved Bus Stop and overwhelmed the store staff with their enthusiastic appreciation of what Bus Stop could do to galvanise their dressing.

And then after the USA and Canada, why not follow with planting Bus Stop in the Far East? By 1979, Bus Stop had opened thirty boutiques all over Japan – and in Hutchinson's in Hong Kong and Metro in Singapore. Toasts were drunk everywhere at the initial launches: sake in Japan, Mai Tai cocktails in Hong Kong and pitchers of the refreshing local Tiger beer in Singapore.

A good time was had by all!

Poster for Hutchinson's, Hong Kong

Bus Stop expands into Grattan mail order between 1976 and 1980

In 1977 Grattan asked me to contribute six pages of my own designs to each issue of their mail order catalogue. This meant choosing each outfit, selecting the best photographer, and superintending and styling each photography session. All my own responsibility!

The invention of mail order was one of the most sophisticated marketing techniques of the 70s. Each season Grattan brought out a new Preview, which allowed the public to 'order' new purchases literally off the page. So girls throughout the country could find out about new trends in their very own home without having to travel to any Bus Stop shop.

Both for Grattan and for Bus Stop, the new joint undertaking became a very valuable new sales success.

Two dresses of jersey and lace (on the left) and embossed velvet (on the right)

The jersey print dress and white wool jacket on the left could be bought separately. The two models wear hats, flowers and jewellery, all of them and many other accessories on sale in our shops.

*Check wool four-piece
made for the Grattan
mail-order catalogue*

Chapter Fifteen

Then and Now

B y 1979 customers could dress exactly as they pleased – mixing styles, brands, designer and street fashions.

To my amazement, the styles of the 70s have returned full circle, and most of the same clothes would not look out of place today. Tea dresses are back, in prints similar to those of the 70s, and seem to be selling like hot cakes.

All lengths of skirt are in, from minis to maxis, as they were in the 70s, and trousers from flares to tight are being worn alternately, depending upon one's mood of the moment.

Today's designers are inspired by yesterday's styles, turning them into relentlessly hip clothing to be worn in the Club culture of today.

Then   *Now*

70s' crepe dress

Same dress, today's girl

Then

70s' printed crepe

As I see it now

Same shape dress with fake red fox fur

Then

Now

70s' tea dress

NOW tea dress

70s' velvet jacket, satin flares, tank top and blouse

Now

Today's version, same jacket with red dress

Close-up of dress

I remember wearing very short black crepe shorts and waistcoat in London for a party in the 70s. Minis and shorts were new and considered to be outrageous; now a party isn't necessary, they can be worn at all times.

The shorts can be worn at any time of the day. Sometimes with thick tights and boots, or with a black see-through top and black shiny or patterned tights, the outfit looking glamorous and exactly as such an outfit would have been worn all those years ago.

Then

Now

70s' shorts and waistcoat

Shorts dress now

Sweaters then were often long tunic styles worn with tight trousers, or were sometimes short and tight.

Then

70s' sweater – then teamed with leggings – is still very Today.

Now

Same sweater, a NOW skirt

Some things may have changed!

I remember that the photo below was taken by *Brides' Magazine* in 1973 (owned by *Vogue*).

The text mentioned that it was 'an answer to the girl who believes in wearing informal dress at her wedding and who prefers a design which she can wear with distinction on the day, and many times afterwards.' The outfit was made in cream crepe, with trousers that were loosely cut Oxford bags, a cream satin blouse tied at the waist, a 40s' type jacket and a cloche hat. Jackets mostly had stiff revers and self-assured shoulders! Very Deauville in the 20s!

This seems to have changed today, as the majority of girls getting married choose to wear more traditional and extremely expensive long white wedding dresses.

Then

Bus Stop bride, c 1974

Now

Same jacket, shorter, and a new ruffled skirt

Then

*One-shoulder
70s' lurex
sweater*

Now

*Stripes as I see
them today*

When one considers that it is thirty-five to forty years ago that we wore these clothes and lived the life, how very little has changed from the way we were.

In fact we all seemed to have more fun then. Living in London, with its great diversity of interests and cultures, it felt like a time of plenty and, as it appeared to me as a young person, relatively problem free. It was a time of no AIDS, unlike today. Sexual activity was less feared. Terrorism was not seen as a continual threat.

Eating out and drinking were relatively cheap. Although most pubs, bars and clubs had an eleven o'clock curfew, we would just take a bottle and go on to people's houses and party into the night.

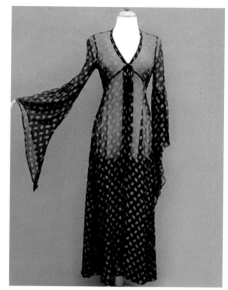

The prices of the clothes in Bus Stop shops were really cheap: in 1969 they started at £2–£3 for dresses and jackets. It is interesting to look at Internet vintage clothing sites and to see Bus Stop clothes at $950 and $485!

Prices in the money-making fashion industry since then have risen astronomically, in part because of increased costs of materials and labour, and in part because of the massive fees demanded by the models and photographers – the top names receive many thousands of dollars a time.

Well, haven't we come a long way!

What shall we wear next?

If I were designing for
BUS STOP today – these
3 styles are what you
might see.

From
Lee Bender
at
Bus Stop